Speak it
BELIEVE IT
RECEIVE IT

HOW TO ALIGN YOUR WORDS WITH THE WORD OF GOD

RONNIE WILSON

Speak It Believe It Receive It

How to Align Your Words with The Word of God

print ISBN: 979-8-35094-856-1
ebook ISBN: 979-8-35094-857-8

CONTENTS

DEDICATION

I would like to dedicate this book to those individuals in my life that I love the most. First and foremost, I thank God for being the head of my life. God, I thank you for being with me every step of the way. All my life, I have always had to lean on and depend on you. You deserve all the glory in my life, and I thank you for keeping me. Even in my worst, you saw fit to love and prosper me; for that, I give your name all the praise. I love you, and I hope to one day to see you face to face.

To my beautiful and supportive mother, Inetia Hardison, I honor and thank you. Mom, you birthed me, and without you, I wouldn't be here today. I am so glad that you were always giving me encouraging words, and I love you for that. I know that there is nothing like a mother's love. You proved that to me firsthand. Mom, just know that this is just the beginning for us. I love you with everything that's in me.

To the **LOVE OF MY LIFE, SHELIA'**, I thank you for all the time and effort you invested in me. We have had some tough times, but you have always seen the best in me. You encourage me daily, and you are a shoulder that I lean on. You are the strength I need when I feel weak. No one affects my life as you do, and *I LOVE YOU*. There is so much more that God has in store for us; just watch God work. My prayer is that I spend my whole life with you. Shelia, I appreciate the wife, mother, friend, and woman of God that you are. I love and honor you for your selflessness, courage, patience, and being my help meet.

I have learned so much from all of you. You are all special to me. I understand how to love in spite of because of you. You are my first ministry. I deeply love and care for you all so much. I pray for you and cover you. I always decree the best for you. May God bless you all abundantly, and may God's favor overtake you. You know, as long as I have breath in my body, I will be there every step of the way. Alesia, Voncile, Kairon, Montez, Danyel, Isaiah, and Serenity. I LOVE YOU, your Dad.

ACKNOWLEDGEMENTS

I thank my heavenly Father for blessing me, and I am forever grateful for all things that you have done. Father, because of you, I was able to weather storms in my life. Father God, you mean so much to me, and I give you all the glory and all the praise. There are many individuals in my life I want to thank for all their encouragement and support. May God add a special blessing to your lives. These individuals are greatly appreciated: Pastor Shelton R Keyes, First Lady Belinda Keyes, and the entire Hickory Grove Disciples of Christ Church family; thank you for your kindness, love, and support. You are an awesome family.

Thank you to the following for your guidance and instruction along this journey, Dr. Prophet Orin Perry, Shepherd Mother Mary E. Perry-Howell, Pastor Shon Speller, Dr. Chemeka Turner Williams, and the entire House of Mandate Inc. Family. Thank you, Bishop Anthony R. Terrell & First Lady Effie Terrell and the Promise Land Church of Christ Family, Bishop Randy Thomas & Apostle Janice Thomas and His Kingdom Ministries, Pastor Ronald Eley & First Lady Angela Eley, and the Lifeline Christian Community Church, Pastor Mae Lilly Andrews and church family, Pastor Carmen Cherry and Impact Life Ministries, Minister Annie Gaynor, Minister Julia Whitehurst, Pastor Larry Caldwell, Prophetess Pugh, and Dr. Reyes. Truly God has placed each of you in my life. I am thankful and appreciate you.

A *SPECIAL ACKNOWLEDGEMENT* to CHURCH ON FIRE MINISTRIES; thank you for your love and support. You are truly a blessing to the body of Christ. I love you with all my heart! #FIRESTARTERS

INTRODUCTION

This book will help you learn how to be blessed by turning negative words into positive ones by aligning our words with the word of God. It will teach you just how powerful God's words are and that we possess that same God-given power. The Bible is God's word, and we believe that when you speak His word, believe it, and receive it into your heart, He will answer your prayers. The word is ready to be used. He left His Word to be a guide and a road map for us to follow. Let us read and reread to get an even better understanding of His Word. Let us have so much word in us that the devil loses his mind trying to figure out how he is going to stop this person. When you have the word, you are a great threat to the enemy. He knows that you can bind his attacks and receive a better outcome. Oh, what a mighty God we serve. We have the victory over the devil. We can do all things through Christ that strengthens us.

I hope that through the Holy Spirit, I will show you ways of conquering the enemy, as well as help you move into your *NEXT LEVEL* in God.

CHAPTER 1

THE POWER OF GODS WORD

The word of god is powerful, and it is also active. It is the key ingredient to knowing what God expects from us, his love for us, and his promises for us. The word of God will guide our lives if we take heed to the instructions that it presents us. The Word will give you guidance directing your understanding like a road map. If you follow its directions, it will surely take you to greater wisdom and understanding. Mostly, it will take you into our Father's loving arms that will be waiting for us in eternity. We need to understand that the promises of God are in His Word. Did you know that every time you read the word of God, you are reading about Jesus? The bible states that He is the word of God. Even in the beginning of time, Christ was there. If you search the scriptures, you will find Him throughout the entire bible. This can only be seen through studying His Word and allowing God to reveal Christ to you. The word of God is so vital to a Christian's life. Knowing the word of God, it can protect you from the enemy's traps and snares. Satan hates it when a Christian is full of the word of God. He knows that if you are full of the word of God, then you are full of Jesus Christ. This defeats him! There is no way he can defeat Christ, so when the Word is in you, he can't defeat you either. The Word of

God is the most powerful weapon known to Christians. The Word of God has created everything in this universe. It has brought kingdoms down, flooded the entire Earth, cast out devils, healed the sick, and even raised the dead.

We as Christians should know that if we have the word of God in us, then we are full of power. We have the power to overcome all circumstances in our life, not only in our life but also in the lives of others. Have you ever been in a situation where it seemed as if you were about to lose your mind? Then right on time, someone came along and gave you a word from God, and after that, you felt like you could go on. The word of God is a restorer; it can fix any problem in your life. We have to speak the Word of God to our problems; we have to stop confessing the problem and start speaking the solution!

The words you speak are powerful. They have the ability to create your reality and transform your life. When you speak something into existence, you are giving that thing power over your thoughts and emotions. You are giving it permission to take up residence in your mind because you have told yourself that it is true. If you say something enough times, eventually, you will start to believe it. When this happens, the world will begin to align itself with that statement until it becomes a reality for you. You are the creator of your world! You have all of the power. You can create anything that you put your mind to! So why not put all your energy into creating a life filled with joy and happiness?

When there was a problem, Jesus spoke the solution to the problem, never the problem. He knew the problem was there, but he knew how to change the negative into the positive. If someone was vexed with a demon, he told it to come out. When you use the word of God against the enemy, it will cause him to flee from you in terror.

If someone was blind, God commanded them to see. We will have what we say! If you are sick and being sick is all you speak of, then you will continue to stay in that condition that you are in! If you are always saying what you don't have, then you will always lack! It is just as simple as that; your healing, deliverance, and financial breakthrough are in your mouth. If you just speak the word of God over your life. I dare you to get in His Word and start saying it daily. You will see things change because the word of God is true, and God cannot lie. Say these words aloud: "I am grateful for my health." "I am grateful for my family." "I am grateful for my home." "I am grateful for my job." "I am grateful for my friends." "I am grateful for my car." Your gratitude will attract more good things into your life! And if something bad happens? Say this instead: "Thank God for this opportunity!"

If God said it, then it is going to happen, but you have to speak it, believe it, and receive it. He wants you to prosper as your soul prospers. You may ask, what is your soul? The soul is the mind, will, and intellect of man, and it houses all of your emotions. The Bible teaches that your thoughts, words, and actions are what define you as a person. Your mind can lead you astray if you don't have knowledge of God or if you don't want to follow the commandments that He has given. The Bible shows us how important it is for us as believers to have our minds in check with God's will so we don't end up like those that have gone astray and lost their way. How does your soul prosper? It prospers through the Word of God.

The more you read, the more God reveals, the more He reveals, and the closer you become to Him. Reading the Word of God is one of the best ways to grow in your relationship with God and to be transformed into the person He created you to be. Isn't' it wonderful that God loves us so much? That He gave us His Word as a weapon to fight the enemy and to change our lives. The Bible is a weapon to fight the enemy of your soul. It is a powerful tool that will help you to overcome all of the temptations and attacks from the devil. You can use it to fight against sin and to encourage yourself when you are feeling down or discouraged. The Word is a sword from God that cuts through the lies of the enemy and gives us the truth. It's not enough to just read it; you have to do it. That means that you need to speak the Word out loud, pray, and meditate on what it says. You can't just read God's Word and then go about your day as if nothing happened.

When you read God's Word, you're giving yourself power over the enemy because he can't stand against God's Word. The Bible says in Ephesians 6:17 that "the sword of the Spirit is the word of God." When you speak or write down the word of God, it has power over sin and death. Reading the Bible will provide you with lifelong teaching, correction, and insights into the heart of God and grow your faith. The Bible will give you hope and show you how much God loves you.

What a mighty God we serve! We must share God's word. When we share this word with unbelievers, it will transform their lives as well. The word of God is just not for us to receive things. We must share this Gospel with all the nations so that souls can be saved. We must let the world know that God still saves, He still heals, and most of all, He is a God of love. He wishes that all the world would accept him as their savior. We must speak the word to the upmost parts of the earth. We have to let every man, woman, boy, and girl know about God's love, the saving power of Jesus Christ, and his death, burial, and his resurrection.

Paul said it best in Hebrews 4:11 "For the word of God is quick, and powerful, and sharper than any two-edge sword, piercing even to the dividing asunder of soul and spirit, and of the joints and marrow, and is a discerner of the thoughts and intents of the heart." Now that in itself is powerful. Paul was explaining that the word is the very force of our being. It is quick, meaning that the word is alive, it is moving, and it is performing everything God sends it out to do. It has the strength to do anything and can never be weakened. The more you use the word of God, the stronger you become. God's Word says it's sharper than any two-edged sword. The Word can go where no other sword could go. It can change you by going to the hidden areas of your life. God knows how you feel, and He even knows your motives, whether good or bad.

When you line up your life with the word of God, you will see things happen, and your life will change. It will do exactly what it says. You just must read it and get it in your spirit. Read it out loud in your hearing so that the word of God can penetrate your soul.

Start believing the word of God. Start confessing it every day. I guarantee when you make the Word of God a habit in your life, it will tear down all of the strongholds of your life. You don't have to be afraid if you have the word of God. It is so good that it covers all bases in your life.

Did you know that there is nothing that the enemy can do that God's word can't cover? I am so glad that Jesus Christ, the Word of God, sealed the deal for us. The Word of God was made flesh and walked with man. He died and paid a debt that none of us was able to pay. Oh, what a mighty God we serve! He has given us access, and he has given us power. We don't have to be weak; we don't have to stay sick; we don't have to be depressed, and we don't have to lack in any area of our lives. God has given us His Word; we must speak and declare the Word. That is our power, the spoken word. The word of God is full of power, and it is up to us to tap into it. The difference between a strong Christian and a weak one is the Word of God. A strong Christian knows what he or she believes and why they believe it. They are able to defend their beliefs with scripture and can put their faith into practice through actions. A weak Christian may have the same beliefs as a strong Christian but does not know why or how to defend them. They cannot back up their faith with scripture, nor can they put it into practice in their life.

Ask yourself, how much word is in you? Let us not forget that the word of God is where the power is. We must speak God's Word in order to defeat the enemy. We win every time we speak God's Word! We must speak it with confidence and not be afraid to use it when needed. We should never believe that we are not able to overcome our enemy because God's Word tells us that we can do all things through Christ Jesus!

When Jesus was in the wilderness being tempted, He never gave the devil an opinion. He gave Satan the word of God. The Word of God is so powerful that it can destroy yolks, heal the broken, and deliver you from any addiction. It is so powerful that it can raise the dead. The Word of God is so powerful that it can make you a new creature in Christ Jesus. It is the Word that will shatter your heart into pieces and then put it back together again, stronger than ever before. It is the Word that will bring you out of the darkest places of your mind and show you that there is hope for tomorrow. The word of God is not just words on paper; it's a living breath inside each one of us. It's a light that shines through even in the darkest of times and never goes out.

We must speak God's Word over our lives daily so that it will become a part of us, covering every area of our lives with His protection and provision. As believers, our words should be filled with His power and authority over everything around us. The Bible says that "death and life are in the power of the tongue," so we must be careful what comes out of it

Through the Word, we are overcomers. We can face all odds against us. We must be grounded and rooted in the Word of God. Reading and studying the Word must be a daily routine in our life.

The body needs physical food to survive, and your soul needs spiritual food to stay spiritually fit. Most people in the natural eat breakfast, lunch, and dinner, and you must do the same with the Word of God. Read it in the morning, make time to read it for lunch, and then read it at night. The more you read, the more you must fight with, and the more power you have to grow. The word of God is the source of all wisdom and the best way to stay grounded in the truth of who Jesus is and what He wants for us.

When you read God's word regularly, you'll be able to hear His voice more clearly and know Him better. When we spend time in His Word, we can better understand ourselves, our needs, and what He wants for us. The Bible is full of amazing stories about people who faced trials and persevered through them with God's help. Reading these stories will encourage you when you're faced with challenges yourself! If you don't read it, you will spiritually die.

I believe that there is nothing worse than a Christian that has access to the word of God and doesn't use it. For example, if someone gives you a million dollars, and you decide not to use the money to buy the basic necessities that you need to survive on a day-to-day basis. That sounds really bad, doesn't it? It is the same thing about the Word of God. If we don't use it, then it will be good for nothing. The Word was made especially for us to use and grow naturally and spiritually. As stated before, it is a road map for our life. We have to know that once we know the promises of God's Word, we are on our way to total victory. Begin to speak God's word, and watch His awesome power change your entire life.

KEYS TO HELP STUDY GODS WORD

- Pray before you begin- Clear your mind of any distractions that life has brought you at that moment and focus on God and His word. Ask him to reveal to you what He wants to teach you.

- Put Yourself in the Scripture- Make this time with God personal. Add your name and see yourself in every word that you read. The word of God is alive and active – relevant still to this day.

- Ask for His guidance and wisdom- Ask God to guide you and give you revelation and understanding as you prepare to read His Word

- Obey the Holy Spirit when He speaks to your heart- Ask God to help you see beyond the words on the page into their deeper meaning. Ask Him to help you understand what is written in such a way that your heart will be changed.

- Search out the truth in His Word through study and prayer.

- Read the Bible in context with other passages of Scripture that relate to the subject being studied.

- Use other Resources- Scholarly commentaries, interlinear Bibles, and Bible handbooks can provide greater insight

Describe how you will be different because of what God has said to you through His Word.

_____

_____

_____

_____

_____

_____

_____

_____

_____

_____

_____

_____

_____

_____

_____

_____

_____

_____

_____

_____

_____

_____

_____

_____

_____

_____

_____

CHAPTER 2

RENEW YOUR MIND

One of the things that I have found out in this Christian walk is that we are in constant spiritual warfare. You see, the enemy never sleeps. There is always a struggle between good and evil. The place where we fight against the enemy the most is in our minds. The mind can be a stumbling block to your Christian walk. When we are young and have not yet learned to properly defend our minds, we are particularly vulnerable to the attacks of others. Others can take advantage of this, and they do so in many ways. One of the most common ways is through words. Words can be used to hurt us or to make us feel like we are worthless or unlovable.

He gets inside of our heads and makes us feel like we can't do anything right. He makes us feel like we're not good enough, like we're worthless, and like we'll never be able to make it in this world. He wants you to believe that there's nothing you can do to change your situation, but he's wrong! There is always something you can do to improve your circumstances, no matter how bad things seem right now. You just need to have faith that you will find a way out of your current situation because God is with you every step of the way.

The definition of the word mind is "the aspect of intellect, and consciousness experienced as combinations of thought, perception, memory, emotion, will, and the imagination." The mind manifests itself subjectively as a stream of consciousness. In other words, the mind can bring into being what it can imagine or what it believes. The enemy starts his attack in the mind. He allows situations to get in your way. His job is to make your problems seem bigger than they appear. You see, everything that the enemy does is only an illusion. Now once you see the illusion and believe it, you put your imagination to work by speaking it into existence. You let the enemy get the victory over you. Basically, we hand over our power to the enemy, but if we can change our mindset, the devil cannot get the victory in our minds. Our minds must be renewed daily by the word of God. We have to adhere to what the Word of God says, and we have to think like God of the Bible. Then and only then will we be able to destroy the enemies' plan against our life. 1Peter 5:8 says it best" Be sober, be vigilant; because your adversary the devil, as a roaring lion, walketh about, seeking whom he may devour" A lion is one that hunts its prey and will destroy anything it encounters. He wants you to believe that your circumstances will always be the same. A defeated mindset will have you believing that you can't be better, that you can't be healed, or that the habit that you have can't be broken. But the devil is a liar! You can overcome every trial and every circumstance just by following God's word and renewing your mind in Christ Jesus. You must speak life over every situation and believe what God says concerning your life. Not only do you have to speak life, but you also must believe and then apply the word of God in your daily walk with him.

There is an old saying that the mind is a terrible thing to waste. If we allow the enemy to continue to occupy space in our minds, no matter what we say, we will lose the battle every time. If we continue to believe the lies of the enemy, we then waste all our God-given power. You see, if we don't use our strength, perseverance, and wisdom, then it is all in vain. Remember, the word of God is a road map and a navigation system for your next destination.

As the body of Christ, we must fight the enemy with the word. It will turn everything in your life that is wrong right. Ask God to help you to renew your mind. Start watching what you say about yourself. Try to think well about yourself. Don't hang around negative people. Surround yourself with people who lift you up.

Don't listen to negative words from people; only say what God says about you. You have the power to move those negative thoughts of the enemy out of your way. The enemy wants us to think that we're not good enough for God or that we don't deserve Him. That's why he uses lies like: "God doesn't love you." Or: "You're too sinful to be a Christian." Or: "You don't have enough faith." Our minds are powerful tools—we can use them for good or evil, but it's up to us which one we choose! If we choose to believe what the enemy tells us about ourselves, then it becomes true for us—and then there's no way out! The enemy will try to make you feel like you're working hard for nothing, that no one is noticing or appreciating what you're doing, and that you're wasting your time on something that's not important. It will tell you that it's too late to start, that someone else is doing it better than you could ever do it, and that the whole world would be better off if you just quit right now. The enemy will say all these things and more, but what it means is this: You are doing exactly what God wants you to do—and He's cheering on your efforts every step of the way! Therefore, we need to resist these lies every time they come into our heads. The good news is that once you start fighting back against these lies, they'll start losing their power over you; they won't be able to control your life anymore!

I encourage you to read everything you can find in the bible about the mind. When your mind is renewed, you have the power to conquer the enemy. I know that this seems hard to do, especially when individuals have hurt you; it seems like the enemy plays those events over and over again in our heads. Give it to God. Because no matter what the devil plays in your head, know that your Heavenly Father will take care of it for you.

We have to be able to fight all the negativity that goes on in our heads. Through the word of God renewing our minds, we can fight and remove our negative motives, feelings, and wrong thoughts. When you read the Bible every day, you'll find yourself feeling more confident in your faith and understanding more about God's plan for your life. You'll find peace when things get tough because you know what God has planned for your future—and it's good! Now that you are more confident and your faith has increased, then you will see miracles in your life.

I know that you are tired of the enemy getting the victory over your life. I know you are tired of the enemy having victory over your relationships, your finances, and your health. You are ready to take back control of your life and get rid of any negative emotions or situations that have been holding you back. The good news is that you can choose to be victorious! Victory is something that you can claim for yourself through the reading of God's Word and renewing of your mind.

When you just get in God's word and start going through the process of renewing your mind, you will see a brand new you. It will be like the light was cut off, and then someone turned on the switch. When the mind is renewed, there is a peace that takes you into a deeper revelation in God. A renewed mind can take you places you thought you could never go. I know people that would rather have peace of mind than money. Only God's word can give you peace of mind. Jesus had this kind of peace of mind. He didn't let anyone disturb his mind. He didn't let people or things turn his mindset from his purpose. We can't allow the enemy to detour us from our destiny. We can have the same mindset as Christ. It is God's will for you to have peace of mind. He doesn't want you to worry about problems. In fact, He just wants you to bring them to Him. We must allow God to help us change the way we think. It is important that we change all the negative mindsets in our life. If not, we will find ourselves in a continual struggle.

The mind is a powerful thing. It can be your greatest asset, or it can be your worst enemy. When you're feeling overwhelmed by the stresses of life, it's easy to find yourself lost in negativity and worry—and that can make you feel like there's no way out. But there is! You don't have to stay trapped in the cycle of negative thoughts that keep you from being happy, fulfilled, and content with your life. With a little bit of faith, trust in God's plan for you will bring you peace in your mind. We have to pull down the strong holds of the mind.

A stronghold is anything that is dominated or occupied by a special group. This is how the enemy gets next to the saints. He tries to overload us with problems and circumstances. His job is to hurt the body of Christ as much as possible and to keep us off focus on our destiny. As we focus on all those things, we lose sight, and the problems create a stronghold for us. Paul said it best in 2 Corinthians 10:4 "For the weapons of our warfare are not carnal, but mighty through God to the pulling down of strong holds."

Through God and His Word, you can speak and take down that warfare that is going on in your head. God is strong and mighty! He is a God who can help us win every battle in our lives! He is a God who gives us strength when we are weak, courage when we are afraid, and hope when all seems lost. Satan tells you that you can't make it, you will never be good enough, you don't have what it takes, you are not loved, you will always be in debt, you will never get rid of that habit, you will never find that mate, and you will never be healed. The devil is a LIAR, and the truth is not in him!

You must know that God loves you. You must know that He has a plan for your life and that He wants to use you in a powerful way. You must know that God will never leave you or forsake you, no matter what happens in your life. You must know that He is the only One who can truly give you peace and joy in your heart. The God of the Bible is the sovereign Ruler of all creation. He is all-powerful and all-knowing, and He has declared in His Word that He will fulfill all His promises to you.

All of God's promises are true, and He is always faithful, even in the midst of trials and hardships. God has promised never to abandon you or leave you alone. He wants you to be free, and he wants you to be healed. He wants to take you places that you could never have dreamed or considered. He wants you to be blessed, and he wants you to prosper. When you focus on the things of God and live in obedience to Him, then the blessings will start coming your way. Your health will improve, you will have more money, and your relationships will improve. It is all in His Word. God's promise is still standing! And it will stand forever! You may not understand exactly how He will keep this promise in your life right now (or even if He will), but His Word says so—so you can rest assured that He will keep his word to you!

It is time to get out of that old mindset. It is time for a new attitude. God has given us the power to pull down the stronghold of the mind. Let us take our minds back. For every time the enemy comes with lies and deception, go to the Word of God. Start speaking right then what God says about you in His Word. Remind the devil that God has the final say and that God is a present help in times of trouble. Just believe God and His Word, and then watch the strongholds of your mind leave. We need to ask God to transform our thoughts and mind into one that is pleasing to Christ. I know if you want to experience God and everything, He has for you, you must be willing to give up the things that are keeping you from going deeper in your relationship with Him.

We can overcome all the negative and toxic thoughts, all of the past things we lost, and even our toxic habits. We can destroy the old mindset and receive a new mind through Christ Jesus. You can make it, and you can win. You are already a winner through Christ. Let us move on and put those former things behind us. Let's move on through God's word. We must continue to stay focused on God's word. We must think and speak like Him. If you do these things, you will be walking with peace of mind. Your mind will be totally free. Then know you can win the battle.

When you let God transform your mind, you are putting your trust in Him to guide you through life. You know that He knows what is best for you and that He has the power to help you overcome any obstacle in your path. When you let Him move forward in you, it means that you are willing to do whatever he wants from this moment forward. You're ready to follow his path without reservation, even if it means leaving things behind or changing direction entirely.

KEYS TO RENEWING YOUR MIND

- Control and Manage Your Thoughts
- Listen/Hear God's Word
- Be Mindful of What You are feeding your mind
- Study the Word of God
- Apply the Word of God
- Speak Truth and Life

- Pray God's Word

SCRIPTURES TO RENEW THE MIND

- Colossians 3:2 Set your minds on things above, not on earthly things

- 1Chronicles 16:15 Be ye mindful always of his covenant; the word which he commanded to a thousand generations.

- Philippians 4:7 And the peace of God, which passeth all understanding, shall keep your hearts and minds through Christ Jesus.

- Ephesians 4:22-24 "to put off your old self, which belongs to your former manner of life and is corrupt through deceitful desires, and to be renewed in the spirit of your minds, and to put on the new self, created after the likeness of God in true righteousness and holiness.

Prayer to Renew Your Mind in God

Father God, renew our minds so that we may be able to understand your ways. I pray that our thoughts are clear to worship you in spirit and truth. Father, set our minds on the things that are above that we may receive from you. Renew our minds and transform our thoughts so that we may think like you, speak like you and walk like you. Father, we thank you for a renewed mind and the strength to carry out the assignments in which you have given. In Jesus' name, we pray.

Why is it important for you to have your mind renewed daily?

Where do you need renewal today? What thoughts seem to plague you? Where do you normally feel negative, insecure, or angry?

_____

_____

_____

_____

_____

_____

_____

_____

_____

_____

_____

_____

_____

_____

_____

_____

_____

_____

_____

_____

_____

CHAPTER 3

TRANSFORM YOUR HEART

In this next chapter, we will discuss matters and issues of the heart. Heart matters can hinder you from your next in God. Heart matters can turn God's ear away from your prayers, and heart matters can keep God's blessings hidden from you. The heart is the most vital organ in the body. It pumps blood through the body to keep it alive. In blood, there is life, but without it, the body won't live. The heart is mentioned 743 times in the Bible. In the Bible, the heart refers to Christians as a person's will or desires. The heart is the center of our being, and it's where our thoughts, feelings, and intentions are born. It's also where our actions originate—and that's why God sees it as the best way to judge whether or not we're doing what he wants us to do. Your heart is a very important part of how you're supposed to live. When God looks at your heart, he sees what kind of person you are. But if he just looks at your actions, he might not see who you really are. Our actions may be visible to everyone else, but they're not always an accurate reflection of what we're thinking and feeling. But when you look at someone's heart, you see everything: their thoughts, their feelings, their intentions—and all of those things are what matter most in God's eyes.

To receive anything from God, He has to see if your motives are pure. Sometimes we want to have things our way without even thinking about what God would have us do. We know that his plan never fails, but we tend to want to rush God. At times it may appear that He doesn't move fast enough for us, but we know that He is an on-time God. In a world where we are surrounded by the darkness of sin, we must take inventory of our own lives and check our hearts to see if it lines up with the Word of God. Let's be honest: we are all human, and that means that we sin. We make mistakes; we say things we don't mean. We fail. And it's not just the big stuff, either—it's the little things too. But the problem with issues of the heart is that it leads us away from God and His plan for our lives. It keeps us from fully experiencing joy and peace because when we're not in line with Him, we can't truly know those things. So how do we fix this? Well, first of all, take inventory of your life. Check your heart to see if it lines up with the word of God. If it doesn't, ask for forgiveness and then turn away from whatever issues have been keeping you from Him.

God judges a person's heart by their motives. We have to make sure that our heart loves God over everything else. According to the bible, a person's heart reveals its true nature. God wants your whole heart. He won't settle for anything less. Your whole heart has to love, need, and want him. Then and only then can He move old things out of your life. We harbor a lot of past issues in our hearts. The bible declares that the heart is deceitful, which means you shouldn't trust your heart. Jesus said where your treasure is, and there will your heart be also. God wants you to be blessed, but what do you want the most? Do you want the gift or to be the giver of the gift? We must search ourselves and see if we have the right motives. If we don't, we must go to God and ask him to take away all things that hinder us from truly loving Him.

Please don't forget that we, first and foremost, should love the Lord our God with all our hearts and our mind. We can't let our hearts detour us from God nor the will of God for our life. We must ask God to give us a pure heart. Isn't it wonderful that God can change our very lives? There is nothing too hard for God. He can take our stony heart and change it to a heart of flesh. All those past issues that dwell in our hearts, he can clean them out and give us a new heart. He can provide us with a heart that will love, a heart that will forgive, and a heart that will trust. It is God's will for us to be like Him. To be like Him, we must read His Word. To be like him, we must ask God to renew our hearts and take out all things, not like Him. Only then can we move in the things of God. The heart doesn't have to be evil. It doesn't have to keep hurting from all the pain of the past. I am so glad we have a heart surgeon, and his name is Jesus Christ. He is a heart fixer and a mind regulator. To God be all the glory. He is able to go into that old heart and fix whatever needs fixing.

You may say no one knows what you've been through. You're right! But I know that God knows what you've been through, and He can fix the problem. All we have to do is trust Him. When He gets in that heart and starts changing things, you are going to be brand new. When God changes your heart, you don't carry yourself the way you used to. You don't act the way you used to, and you don't talk the way you used to. He brings on a brand-new change. So, I encourage you to look at God's word and see what it says about the heart. Meditate on the Word and start speaking the word aloud in your hearing. Confess that Word out loud and see the manifestation of God's word penetrate your life. It will change you; it will take you higher in God.

God wants your heart to be right so you can have a full relationship with him. He loves you and only wants the best for you. He doesn't want you to be happy here on earth, but He has a place for you in heaven. Only the pure in heart shall see God. So, we can't let our heart or the enemy put those things in us to deceive us from the promises of God. So, guard your heart, and be careful what you let in it. Don't let the devil tell you otherwise. You are a child of God. You will love God above everything else in your life. You know that He has restored you and that you are in constant fellowship with Him. We know that with God, nothing is impossible. I have been there before; I had a lot of past issues in my life. I am glad to say that the Lord helped me through my hurts and pains. I thank God for deliverance. At the time, I didn't understand why people had to leave, why some of my family members didn't like me, and why people would intentionally hurt me with their words. Jesus came to heal the hurt. It took time. The enemy wanted me to dwell on the same old negative thoughts and past pains. He wanted to keep me in bondage. You see, when the heart is full of bitterness, pain, and unforgiveness, it is hard for you to even focus on God. That is a distraction of the enemy, and that's what he wants us to do, have a heart that is filled with malice that we can't be postured right in God.

It doesn't matter what the enemy is trying to do or deceive you into thinking; let God come on in and fix that heart. You can never tap into the full potential of love and blessings harboring the wrong thing in your heart.

God wants you to prosper in all you do. He truly loves His children, and He is always willing to make way for them. We must remember that He wants us not just to be blessed, but He also wants us to live right. In that, the heart must be right with God. If there are some things that you are holding in your heart, I want you to release them to God right now. Say this prayer and focus on God. I want you to give it all to him right now. Give every area of hurt, pain, strife, jealousy, malice, and envy to God.

KEYS TO TRANSFORMING THE HEART

- Forgiveness Quickly

- Repent Often

- Give Your Burdens and Troubles to God

- Ask God to cleanse your heart

- Pray that God gives you a heart after Him

- Study and meditate on His Word daily

SCRIPTURES TO TRANSFORMING THE HEART

- **Ezekiel 36:26:** I will give you a new heart and put a new spirit within you; I will remove your heart of stone and give you a heart of flesh.

- **Psalm 139:23-24:** Search me, God, and know my heart; test me and know my concerns. See if there is any offensive way in me; lead me in the everlasting way.

- **Psalm 51:10:** God, create a clean heart for me and renew a steadfast spirit within me.

- **Philippians 1:6:** I am sure of this, that He who started a good work in you will carry it on to completion until the day of Christ Jesus.

- **Proverbs 3:5:** Trust in the Lord with all your heart, and do not rely on your understanding.

PRAYER TO TRANSFORMING THE HEART

Father God, I come to you in the name of Jesus Christ. Oh God, let the living waters of your Word spring up in the hearts of your people reading this prayer. Let the winds of your Holy Spirit wash and blow away all the dirty parts of the heart. Create in us a clean heart worthy and satisfying to you. Let it take away every hurt, bad motive, and let it be renewed in Christ Jesus. Circumcise our hearts that we follow your every word and love you more than anything else in our lives. In Jesus' name, I pray, Amen!

What will a transformed heart mean to you?

_____

_____

_____

_____

_____

_____

_____

_____

_____

_____

_____

_____

_____

_____

_____

_____

_____

_____

_____

_____

_____

_____

_____

_____

_____

_____

_____

_____

What does knowing these things mean to you?

_____

_____

_____

_____

_____

_____

_____

_____

_____

_____

_____

_____

_____

_____

_____

_____

_____

_____

_____

_____

_____

_____

_____

_____

_____

_____

_____

CHAPTER 4

TURN FEAR INTO FAITH

One of the major tools that the devil comes against us with is FEAR. Just saying the word alone can put it in some of the hearts of God's people. God doesn't want us to fear anything the enemy tries to do in our lives. The definition of fear is a distressing emotion induced by a perceived threat. It is a basic survival mechanism occurring in response to a specific stimulus, such as pain or the threat of danger. In short, it is the ability to recognize danger and flee from it or confront it.

To be afraid of something is to have a fear of it. Well, the devil uses this tool oh so well. As a matter of fact, that is what he plays with the most, your fears. His job is to take you off of the assignment that God has for you. He brings up all kinds of circumstances in your life. He knows that if he can just detour you from serving God, he will have victory over you. How many people know that the devil is a liar? We have a God that is fearless, and therefore we need to be too! How can we be fearless? By operating in faith!

As we continue along this journey of spiritual growth as well as personal growth, we are surely to find ourselves in moments that provoke fear and in situations where we will be face to face with fear itself. Life is full of possibilities that may bring these feelings upon us and the thoughts of negative situations that could or could not possibly happen. As believers, we can't focus on the what-ifs of the world or all the possible negative outcomes that could happen. Sometimes, we can be afraid of what might happen. But that's no reason to let fear hold you back. You can turn your fears into strengths by knowing that you are capable of achieving whatever it is that you want, no matter how hard it might seem. Fear is a natural, normal response that can be helpful in some cases. But it's important to remember that fear is not the only way to respond to a situation. Fear can be so powerful that it can stop you from taking action or making decisions—even when those decisions are the right ones. So how do you turn fear into faith?

It's all about taking a step back and looking at your fears objectively. Are they really rational? Do they really have merit? Or is there something else going on beneath the surface? When you're able to look at your fears this way, it becomes easier for you to make better decisions and take action more confidently. God's ultimate goal is intimacy with us and our total dependence on Him to sustain us. When we focus on Jesus and our faith in Him, we learn to lean and depend on him. Therefore, when these feelings of fear arise, we know that God has given us the power to conquer and overcome. Overcoming the spirit of fear with faith helps our spirit grow stronger in our spiritual and personal walk, and we become more confident in who we were called to be.

Fear can be paralyzing. But with faith, you can turn your fear into something powerful. You have to believe in yourself. You must believe in your abilities and that you're capable of achieving whatever it is that you want. You have to know that the path will be difficult, but it will also be rewarding and fulfilling.

You see, faith is the opposite of fear. Either you will have one or the other. You will either believe God for something, or you won't; it is as simple as that! First, to stop the enemy from causing you to fear, you must get into the word of God and find out what God says about fear. God wants you to know that he didn't give you the spirit of fear. God wants you to trust him through everything that may be going on in your life. There is no need to be afraid because our God can do anything. We know in God's word that we can speak to our fears.

We don't have to sit here and worry about our problems. You see, a lot of us, because of fear, have missed out on a lot of God's blessings. He gave us a dream; we are afraid to take that leap of faith to get it. He gave gifts, but we are afraid to step out and use them. We allow our fears to hinder us, and God is trying his best to get us into a greater, much more rewarding place. So we get comfortable with where we are and don't want to further ourselves. This leaves any gift that God has given us dormant and desolate. Then we wonder why we are struggling so much; it is because we won't move. We have allowed the enemy to hinder how God wants to move in our life. We must speak the word of God, believe it, and then receive the blessings that God has for us. It is according to your faith! You have to cast aside all manner of fear in your life. Then you must let your faith take over and watch God move on your behalf.

Fear can stop a lot of things from happening in our lives. We must tear down the stronghold of fear. I can personally recall some of the things I feared the most. I used to fear what people thought about me. I used to fear being alone. I used to fear not being accepted, but through the love of Jesus Christ, I have found that it doesn't matter.

If God is for me, then who can be against me? We have to let the enemy know that he has no victory. When we decide to believe in God with all of our hearts, then we can overcome any obstacle that the devil can throw at us!

We can stand against the enemy, or we can lie down and let him run over us. We have the authority and power to stop the enemy. Let us fight the devil in all we do. Let us remove fear from our vocabulary. You can win; you can be all that God wants you to be.

Fear is not an option. Don't forget that the power is in your mouth. Speak the Word of God, believe the word of God, and watch and receive the blessing. There are so many ways that the devil would love to stop the body of Christ. We have to know that the devil is already defeated, and we have a God that can take away all of our fears. Trust in him, and he will never leave us nor forsake us.

We do not have the spirit of fear. We are mighty in God, and there is no devil in hell that can keep us in fear once we know who we are and who we serve. Our God is able to chase away all our fears and draw us close to His Word. Keep His Word close to your heart. Please meditate on His Word Day and night. Let God's Word transform your fear into faith. You will have an abundance of blessings in your life. Real courage comes from facing your fears with faith. Faith is not the absence of fear but the presence of hope. Even when you face uncertainty, God wants to give you courage and peace. As you trust Him, He will increase your faith and help you to overcome your anxiety. Remember what faith means—it means belief without proof! You don't have to prove that something will happen for it to happen. Faith is believing in what can't be proven but knowing there's still a chance for good things to happen anyway!

KEYS TO OVERCOMING FEAR AND ACTIVATE YOUR FAITH

- **Pray for courage and strength!** Find a quiet place and talk with God about your fears and concerns; he'll help give you clarity on what they mean and how to overcome them.

- **Acknowledge and try to understand your fear.** Is it logical, is it possible, and/or is it probable?

- **Pray for guidance, wisdom, and knowledge about your situation!**

- **Read the Bible!** Read scriptures about people who overcame their fears. This might sound like an old-fashioned suggestion, but the Bible is full of stories where people faced their fears head-on and came out stronger on the other side—it's chock-full of inspiration for us all!

- **Get support!** Talk with your friends about how they've dealt with their fears, or find a group or mentor who can offer guidance as you work through yours.

- **Listen to worship music or sermons!** You can have a deeper faith in your life. Many people think they don't have time to create more space for God and His Word, but we know that's not true! All it takes is one little change: listening to praise and worship music throughout the day.

- **Take action!** We all have things we're afraid of doing, —but if we don't do them, our lives will never change for the better, and you will never know what your NEXT will be.

- **Stay around those who BELIEVE!** Talk to someone who has faith in you and believes in you, so they can strengthen, encourage and push you to keep going and have faith that it is ALREADY done!

- **Remember that God is with you!** No matter what happens, God will never leave you no forsake you. Even when you feel alone, you must know that He is walking with you every step of the way.

SCRIPTURES TO FIGHT FEAR

- Psalm 54:4 In God I will praise his word, in God I have put my trust, I will not fear what flesh can do unto me.

- So be strong and courageous! Do not be afraid, and do not panic before them. For the Lord, your God will personally go ahead of you. He will neither fail you nor abandon you." Deuteronomy 31:6 NLT

- "I have told you all this so you may have peace in me. Here on earth, you will have many trials and sorrows. But take heart because I have overcome the world." John 16:33 NLT

- Though a mighty army surrounds me, my heart will not be afraid. Even if I am attacked, I will remain confident." Psalm 27:3 NLT

- Isaiah 35:4 Say to them that are of a fearful heart, Be strong, fear not: behold, your God will come with a vengeance, even God with a recompense; he will come and save you.

- Luke 12:4 And I say unto you my friends, Be not afraid of them that kill the body, and after that have no more that they can do.

- Proverbs 3: 25-26 Be not afraid of sudden fear, neither of the desolation of the wicked when it cometh. For the Lord shall be thy confidence and shall keep thy foot from being taken.

PRAYER TO FIGHT AGAINST FEAR

Father, in the name of Jesus, we thank you for not giving us the spirit of fear but one of faith and Holy Boldness. Let us always remember that when the enemy comes to destroy us that we have the Word of God that will conquer all of our fears. We stand in Faith and Power. Fear has no jurisdiction over our lives. We thank you for allowing us to overcome every thought that's hindering us from operating fully in Power. Thank you for giving us the victory over all fears. We bless your Holy name. Amen!

What are you fearful of?

What truth about God gives you courage during the fear?

_____

_____

_____

_____

_____

_____

_____

_____

_____

_____

_____

_____

_____

_____

_____

_____

_____

_____

_____

_____

_____

_____

_____

_____

_____

_____

_____

CHAPTER 5

WALKING BY FAITH

As you navigate through life, it's important to remember one thing: You cannot see what your journey has in store. But it is possible that if you trust God and follow His guidance, you will reach your destination. The journey of faith is a walk of sight. You can't see what lies ahead, but you trust God to lead and guide you. We're reminded in 2 Corinthians 5:7 that we walk by faith and not by sight. But wait, what exactly does walking by faith look like?

When we walk by sight, we are focused on the things that are right in front of us—the obstacles that block our path, the things keeping us from moving forward. We focus on everything that could go wrong and how hard it will be to overcome those obstacles. This type of thinking can lead to despair and discouragement because it assumes that there is no way out of our current situation. When we walk by faith, however, we believe that God has a plan for our lives—and that plan includes success! When we walk by faith and not by sight (Hebrews 11:1), we are able to see beyond the obstacles in front of us and into the future. We recognize that God wants us to succeed—and He will help us get there! Have you ever had moments where you may have been discouraged by what you see, and doubt sinks in? Or have you ever walked down the street and suddenly realized that you're lost. Maybe you're not even sure where you started from. What do you do? Do you start walking in circles, hoping to somehow find your way back? Do you call up a friend who knows the area better than you do and ask them for directions? Or do you just give up and go home? If only it were that easy! If only we could look at our phones or ask someone else for help and be done with it—then we'd all be fine. When you're lost, it's hard to know where you started from or what direction to go in. There are times when we are unfamiliar with our surroundings. Some people feel overwhelmed by this unfamiliar territory and choose to turn back.

But what if there were another option? What if there was a third option: one that allowed us to keep walking without knowing where we'd end up but still trusting that God would lead us to our destination in His time? This is what it means to walk by faith and not by sight. Even though we can't see what's going on around us, we have faith that God will guide us as long as we keep moving forward toward Him. We must have faith that God will guide us as long as we keep moving forward toward Him. It's not always easy, but this is the only way to live: trusting in His plans for us even when we can't see where they might lead. Faith is the belief in something that we cannot see or prove. It is confidence in the unseen.

We must live each day by faith, even though we cannot see what is ahead of us. We choose to trust God's promises, even though they are not always visible to our eyes. Faith is the surest way to live an abundant life here on earth. This is a difficult lesson to learn because it is so easy to believe that our circumstances are the most important thing in the world. We can become so focused on what is happening around us that we forget about God's plan for our lives – and how He will use us to accomplish His purposes. But if we look at this principle from a different perspective, it can be an incredibly freeing thing. Most of us would much rather have faith than sight – because having faith means that we don't have to worry about whether or not something will happen! Instead, we just trust in God's Word and allow Him to work in our lives as He sees fit.

It is easy to get caught up in the daily grind of life and lose sight of God's bigger plan for us. It is also easy to forget how fleeting this life is and how much more valuable eternal life with Christ is. When we walk by faith, we do not base our lives on what we see in this world. Instead, we base our lives on God's Word and what He has promised us for our future. When we walk by faith and not by sight, we remember that our lives are temporary—and that there is so much more awaiting us after death.

KEYS TO STRENGTHENING YOUR FAITH

- Pray and meditate on the word of God daily.

- Read and study the Word of God.

- Be transparent with God

- Attend church services on a regular to hear the Preached Word

- Make sure you surround yourself with and spend time with other believers in Christ so that you can be strengthened by their faith and their love for God.

- Persevere through trials and tribulations

- Listen to testimonies about answered prayers and miracles

SCRIPTURES TO INCREASE YOUR FAITH

- **Romans 8:38-39** "For I am sure that neither death nor life, nor angels nor rulers, nor things present nor things to come, nor powers, nor height nor depth, nor anything else in all creation, will be able to separate us from the love of God in Christ Jesus our Lord.

- **Philippians 1:6** "And I am sure of this, that he who began a good work in you will bring it to completion at the day of Jesus Christ."

- **Mark 11:22-24** "And Jesus answered them, "Have faith in God. Truly, I say to you, whoever says to this mountain, 'Be taken up and thrown into the sea,' and does not doubt in his heart but believes that what he says will come to pass, it will be done for him. Therefore I tell you, whatever you ask in prayer, believe that you have received it, and it will be yours."

- **Ephesians 3:20** "Now to him who is able to do far more abundantly than all that we ask or think, according to the power at work within us."

PRAYER TO INCREASE YOUR FAITH

Father, in the name of Jesus, we thank you for allowing us to have Faith. We know that in your Word, you stated that every man had been given a measure of Faith. We thank you for the increase of faith; we thank you for the understanding of your Word that we may grow stronger in you and who you have called us to be. Continue to keep our eyes focused and stay on the things above, for we know that the things of this world are only temporary. We thank you, God, for all that you have done and will continue to do.

What circumstances or fears are you facing that have made you stop praying or even paralyzed you in your spiritual growth?

_____

_____

_____

_____

_____

_____

_____

_____

_____

_____

_____

_____

_____

_____

_____

_____

_____

_____

_____

_____

_____

_____

_____

_____

_____

Who in your life needs you to deepen your faith so that you can help them navigate through their journey in life?

_____

_____

_____

_____

_____

_____

_____

_____

_____

_____

_____

_____

_____

_____

_____

_____

_____

_____

_____

_____

CHAPTER 6

WALKING IN FAVOR

The favor of God is a blessing and a gift, one that must be received with gratitude and humility. It is not something that can be earned or deserved but rather something which is bestowed upon us by the grace of our God. God's favor is something we all seek, for it is the key to our success. We should not be asking for God's favor because we want to be successful, but rather because we want to do what God wants us to do. Favor is one of the most powerful weapons that God has given us. Again it's a blessing and gift from God that gives you protection, strength, and wisdom to do what you need when you need it. If we ask for His favor, he will give it to us.

Do you know that you have favor with God? You may ask what exactly is favor. Favor is an attitude of approval or liking, an act of kindness beyond what is due or usual. It is having God's undeserving, unmerited blessings surround you like a force field. Sometimes we think favor means money. It is more than money. Favor has God in your life. He is the one that is the giver of all blessings. Favor also covers every part of your life. Favor can take you farther than material things. It goes where your ability can't go. So what does it mean when we say that God has given us favor? It means He has put His stamp of approval on us—He sees something special in us—and He's going to work through us for His glory!

The favor of God is the most valuable treasure one can possess in life. It is something that you should not take lightly because it will lead you to a wonderful life. The favor of God will give you the opportunity to succeed in all that you do, and it will help you get through any difficult situation. The favor of God is something that every believer wants to have, but only those who have worked hard for it will be able to acquire it. It is important for believers to know how they can acquire this precious gift from God so they can be blessed with His grace and mercy throughout their lives. It is a gift that we do not deserve, and yet it is offered freely to us by our Lord. The favor of God provides us with true peace and joy that cannot be found in any other place. It allows us to rest in Him and know that He is always there for us. When we think of the word "favor," we often think about it as being something that only happens when other people help us out or give us things. But it's not just about other people—it's about God's favor on us! He wants us to live our lives in such a way that His blessing is felt by everyone around us, including ourselves.

We all know that God is our source of all good things, but what many people don't realize is that God gives us favor with man as well. God gives you favor with man, and favor goes out and prepares the way. It will have you in the right places at the right times. When you have favor with someone, that person wants to help you or give you something. They see something in you that makes them want to be generous toward you. Favor is like an invisible shield that protects us from the attacks of Satan and the world, and it gives us confidence that God will provide for our needs, even when we don't know how He will do it.

The favor of God with man is the favored relationship that God has developed with mankind. This relationship is a two-way street, and it is the desire of God to share His love with us. The favor of God with man is a blessing from Him. It is something we can never earn or deserve but only accept as a gift from above. The favor of God is not contingent upon our faithfulness or obedience, but rather it is bestowed upon us by grace alone (see Ephesians 2:8-9). It does not mean that we should expect special treatment from God or others; rather, it means that we are called to spread His love to others in order to help them see His light and goodness in their lives as well. So how do we know if we have God's favor? The Bible tells us that "the righteous will live by faith" (Romans 1:17). This means that if we are trusting in Jesus Christ as our Savior, then we can be confident that God has given us His favor in all areas; of our lives! We don't have to worry about losing it either, because once we have it—we've got it for good!

God has given you favor in your finances. You shall be prosperous. God has blessed you with the ability to be prosperous, and He will continue to bless you if you ask Him. The Bible says that God will not withhold any good thing from those who walk uprightly (see Psalm 84:11). Proverbs 10:22 says that a good man leaves an inheritance for his children's children, but a sinner's wealth is stored up for the righteous. Because God has given you favor in your finances, you can expect that His blessings will continue to flow into your life. Because He has blessed you, He wants to give you even more, more than you can think or imagine!

There is more that God desires you to have. Not only does He want you financially favored, but He also came that you would have life and life more abundantly. Favor does all these things. The enemy does not want you to know you have favor with God. Nevertheless, you have to speak those words out of your mouth. Every morning you should speak God's favor over your life. Speak it over your marriage, over your finances, over your job, over your children, over your pastor, over your church, over your country, and your world. Let the enemy know that God has given you the power, and that power can create a good situation out of a bad one. Watch God's favor take over and destroy the plans of the enemy. What the devil meant for bad, God has designed for your good. Speak it out over your life and watch favor surround you like a shield. Isn't it good that God loves us enough that He grants favor to his children? Favor was given to us when Jesus died on the cross. When you are a believer, the favor of God is all over you. Favor brings prosperity, and prosperity brings everything else with it.

So how do we get this favor? It's simple: we must have a relationship with God. When we have a relationship with God and ask him for his blessing on us, he gives it freely and without hesitation because he loves us so much! When you have the favor of God and man, there are many benefits: You will be protected from those who would seek to harm you or your family, your business will grow and prosper, you will be successful in whatever endeavor you pursue, and people will want to be around you because they see your light shining through.

God wants you to have favor in every area of your life. He wants you to live a life that is full of blessings and success, and He has given us the power to do that.

We are all familiar with the scripture in Romans 12:16, "Live in harmony with one another; do not be haughty, but associate with the lowly; do not claim to be wiser than you are." We also know God wants us to treat others well and love others as ourselves (Matthew 22:39). But what does it mean to have favor in every area of our lives?

If we are living righteously before Him, we should expect His blessing in all areas of life—our relationships with family members, coworkers, and friends; our finances; even our health! The more faithful we are to His teachings and laws, the more blessings He will give us.

KEYS TO OBTAINING FAVOR

- Be submitted unto God and follow His commandments
- Love Gods and Gods People
- Have an intimate relationship with God
- Give your tithes, offerings, and gifts
- Honor and respect
- Humility
- Be Faithful and Consistent
- Praise God at all times and through all things
- Obtain the Wisdom of God and grow in understanding

SCRIPTURES ON THE FAVOR OF GOD

- **Psalm 5:12** For thou, LORD, wilt bless the righteous; with favor wilt thou compass him as with a shield.

- **Genesis 18: 3** And said, My Lord, if now I have found favor in thy sight, pass not away, I pray thee, from thy servant.

- **Luke 2: 52** And Jesus increased in wisdom and stature, and in favor with God and man.

- **Proverbs 16: 15** In the light of the king's countenance is life, and his favor is as a cloud of the latter rain.

- Psalm 90:17. Let the favor of the Lord our God be upon us, and establish the work of our hands upon us; yes, establish the work of our hands!

PRAYER TO OBTAIN GODS FAVOR

Father, in the name of Jesus, we thank you for who are. Today we pray for the favor of God to rest in and on our lives. Father, we thank you for giving us the gift of favor so that we may Glorify your name. Father, we pray that through our faith in you that you continue to allow the favor of God and the favor with men. We praise you in advance for all that you continue to do.

List and describe five ways that God has demonstrated unmerited favor in your life.

_____

_____

_____

_____

_____

_____

_____

_____

_____

_____

_____

_____

_____

_____

_____

_____

_____

_____

_____

_____

_____

_____

_____

_____

_____

_____

_____

_____

_____

_____

How are you positioning yourself to experience God's favor?

_____

_____

_____

_____

_____

_____

_____

_____

_____

_____

_____

_____

_____

_____

_____

_____

_____

_____

_____

_____

_____

_____

_____

_____

_____

CHAPTER 7

THE POWER OF SPEAKING LIFE

Proverbs 18:20-21 states, "*From* the fruit of their mouth a person's stomach is filled; with the harvest of their lips, they are satisfied. The tongue has the power of life and death, and those who love it will eat its fruit." To speak life is to be a person of hope, edification, and blessing to others through what you say. The power of words is something that often goes unnoticed. You are not a negative naysayer who only speaks about the negative things in life. You are not a gossip who only speaks negatively about others. You are not a person who speaks words of condemnation and judgment. Instead, you speak words that build up and encourage others.

When you speak life, you are speaking God's word into the lives of people around you. The Bible says that God's word is a lamp unto our feet (Psalm 119:105). That means that when we read His word, it lights up our path so we can walk confidently in the direction He has for us. When we speak life, we help others find their path by pointing them toward the truth of God's word and showing them how it works in their lives.

When we speak life into someone else, we are helping them see the good in themselves and their situation—even if it isn't obvious at first glance. When we speak life into someone else, we are giving them hope where there was none before—hope is one of the most important things in this world! We believe everyone has something they can offer the world—a unique perspective, experience, or skill set that can benefit someone else. But sometimes, we're afraid to share our gifts because we think no one will notice them or care. That's where you come in! When you're able to be a voice for Christ in your workplace, community, family, and friends, it allows those around you to see how much God loves them and wants to use them for His glory.

The words you choose, the words you say, and the words you write are all-powerful. In fact, they can be so powerful that they can change your life and the lives of others forever. We should be very careful with what we say because this is how we can either give life or take it away. When we speak life, it gives hope and encouragement; when we speak death, it brings despair and discouragement. This is why it is important for us to speak life in situations where there is none, as well as not speak death in situations where there is life.

For example: if someone has a broken leg, you could say, "You're never going to walk again," but this would cause them to despair because their leg will heal, and they will walk again one day soon! However, if you said, "You'll be able to walk again soon," this would give hope that they will one day walk again, which gives encouragement for them to continue healing their broken leg until it's completely healed so that they can walk once again!

Those who purpose to speak life understand the power of their words. They understand that their words have consequences, and they are willing to take responsibility for those consequences. When we speak life, we are speaking truth and light into dark places. When we speak life, we are making an impact that will last for generations to come. Those who desire to be used by God in this way must pray daily for discernment and wisdom concerning their words. They must learn how to build up instead of tear down, how to encourage instead of discouraging, and how to give hope instead of despair.

KEYS TO SPEAKING LIFE

- Speak God's Word over your life daily
- Speak affirmations and declarations that align with the Word of God.
- Speak words of encouragement to yourself, your spouse, your children, your job, and about the situations in your life
- Speak words of praise and gratitude

SCRIPTURES TO SPEAKING LIFE

- **Proverbs 18:21** Death and life are in the power of the tongue: and they that love it shall eat the fruit thereof.
- **Phil 4:8** Whatever things are true, whatever things are noble, whatever things are just, whatever things are pure, whatever things are lovely, whatever things are of good report, if there is any virtue and if there is anything praiseworthy—meditate on these things.
- **Matt 21:22** And whatever you ask in prayer, you will receive, if you have faith.
- **Isaiah 55:11** So shall my word be that goes out from my mouth; it shall not return to me empty, but it shall accomplish that which I purpose, and shall succeed in the thing for which I sent it

- **Mark 11:23** Truly, I say to you, whoever says to this mountain, 'Be taken up and thrown into the sea,' and does not doubt in his heart, but believes that what he says will come to pass, it will be done for him.

- **Matt 4:4** But he answered, "It is written, "'Man shall not live by bread alone, but by every word that comes from the mouth of God.'"

PRAYERS TO SPEAKING LIFE

Father, we come to you in the name of Jesus. It is spoken in your word that we can speak those things not as though they were. Father God, thank you for giving us the power of the tongue. We cancel every attack of the enemy in our lives and every place where the enemy has told us that we will never be. Father, we speak life to every dead situation or dream. We speak that we shall live again in be strong in the power of your love and might. We rejuvenate every dry place in our lives, and there will be life and life more abundantly in Jesus' name

What does it mean to you to speak life?

_____

_____

_____

_____

_____

_____

_____

_____

_____

_____

_____

_____

_____

_____

_____

_____

_____

_____

_____

_____

_____

_____

_____

_____

_____

_____

What are your daily affirmations that you speak to command your day?

_____

_____

_____

_____

_____

_____

_____

_____

_____

_____

_____

_____

_____

_____

_____

_____

_____

_____

_____

_____

_____

_____

CHAPTER 8

BELIEVING GODS WORD

To believe in God is to believe that He is and that His Word is true. According to Scripture, there is power in believing and in speaking the word of God in our everyday lives in whatever situation we face. 2 Corinthians 4:13 says,

"I believed, and therefore I spoke," We also believe and therefore speak. When we speak the truth about who God is, what He has done for us, and what He wants to do with us, He can work through us to bless others. But when we don't believe God's word for what it is, we get caught up in believing the lies of the world. In Galatians 6:7, Paul says that the truth will set us free. The truth is found in God's word, and when we believe it, we are set free from believing lies.

If you believe in God in the Word of God, there is Power in that alone. If you believe that Jesus Christ is the Son of God and rose from the dead, you can be successful in every area of your life. If you believe that God loves you and has a purpose for your life, you can overcome the mistakes of the past. If you believe that God wants to use your talents, abilities, and passions to fulfill His destiny for your life, then He will give them to you. The power of what we believe is incredible.

The Bible says in Jeremiah 29:11, "For I know the plans I have for you," declares the Lord, "plans to prosper you and not harm you, plans to give you hope and a future." This means that even though things may seem bad right now—even though things may seem like they won't ever get better—God has plans for us! He knows about our pasts and our mistakes; He doesn't want us to keep repeating those same mistakes over again! He wants us to move forward into the future with

Sometimes I know that it's hard to believe in something that you can't see. It's hard to trust in a God who is so far away and who seems to have abandoned you. But if you really believe in God, you truly believe that God is, you wholeheartedly believe that God's Word is true, and believe that nothing is hidden that will not be revealed—then you have nothing to fear. There are no secrets between you and God. There are no lies or half-truths left. Everything has been made known, and everything has been forgiven. If this is true for you—that all of your sins have been forgiven, all of your wrongs have been made right—then stop worrying about what may or may not happen tomorrow. Stop worrying about what might happen next year. Instead, focus on today, and live in the present moment with all its joys and sorrows, its victories and defeats, its ups and downs. Live each day as though it were your last—because it very well could be!

The Bible is the living, active word of God. It is a lamp to our feet and a light to our path (Psalm 119:105). God's Word is powerful enough to create, but it

is also powerful enough to sustain life. It can not only create something out of nothing, but it can also bring dead things back to life again. In the book of John, chapter 5, verse 21, Jesus says: "I am the resurrection and the life; he who believes in me will live even if he dies, and everyone who lives and believes in me will never die."

The Bible says that the Word of God is the source of all truth. It's not just a collection of words but a living, breathing entity that speaks to us and changes our lives when we listen. We believe that by reading and understanding this Word, we can learn how to live our lives according to God's instructions.

KEYS TO BELIEVING GODS WORD

- Read and study God's Word every day.

- Pray about it each day, asking God to show you how to apply it to your life.

- Tell someone else what you've learned from the Bible that day—it helps you remember it better!

- Build a habit of memorizing Scripture so that it becomes a part of who you are as a Christian

- Trust God and his promises because he is faithful to keep them.

SCRIPTURES TO BELIEVING GODS WORD

- **John 14:1** Do not let your hearts be troubled. You believe in God; believe also in me.

- **Matthew 21:22** And all things you ask in prayer, believing, you will receive.

- **John 20:29** Jesus said to him, "Because you have seen Me, have you believed? Blessed are they who did not see and yet believed."

- **Mark 9:23 And** Jesus said to him, "'If You can?' All things are possible to him who believes."

- **1 Peter 1:8** And though you have not seen Him, you love Him, and though you do not see Him now, but believe in Him, you greatly rejoice with joy inexpressible and full of glory.

PRAYERS TO BELIEVING GODS WORD

Father, we come to you in the name of Jesus, and we decree and declare that your word is true. You are a God that will not lie. We thank you that not only is your word true, but it is full of power. We need your glory, and the only way we can get it is by understanding you. Give us God's true revelation of you. Let us taste and see that you are good. Direction comes from your word. Deliverance comes from your word. Love and peace come from your word; let's meditate day and night to get an even greater relationship with you and your word in Jesus' name.

Do you struggle with believing the promises of God as written in his Word?

How did you overcome our areas of unbelief? What steps did you take?

_____

_____

_____

_____

_____

_____

_____

_____

_____

_____

_____

_____

_____

_____

_____

_____

_____

_____

_____

_____

_____

_____

_____

_____

_____

CHAPTER 9

ENCOURAGE YOURSELF IN THE LORD

Have you ever felt defeated? Have you ever felt as if no one understands you? Have you ever felt that there was no one in your corner to strengthen you after you have given all of yourself to help others? Have you ever been to the point that nothing that you try seems to work? When nothing else will work, be like David in the Bible, and encourage yourself in the Lord. Do it with the word of God. In this portion of the book, we are going to talk about encouraging yourself. You are a child of God. You are loved and cherished by God, who gave you the best gift He could possibly give: His own life.

Think back to the last situation, and it seemed like you were all alone. Do you remember searching for someone to give you an answer, but no one was there? That is when you have to encourage yourself. Encourage means to give support, confidence, or hope to someone. When you are going through hardships, trials, pain is knocking at your door, and the devil is up to his tricks, you have to have enough confidence in the Word of God. When you encourage yourself by what God says about you, you will have the strength to weather the storms of life. Certain situations may come, and it will take you to encourage yourself in the word of God. You mustn't always rely on people to be there. We often want support, but it is not always given. One thing is for sure; God's word will always encourage you. He said he would never leave you nor forsake you. God's word is always there.

When situations come up in your life, speak the word of God and encourage yourself in him. Remember that the real power is in your mouth. Death and life are in the power of the tongue. Don't worry about what people do or say about you. Always speak what God says about you. Speak life and encourage yourself. You are more than a conqueror through Christ Jesus. You are the head and not the tail. Prophesy over your life. Speak and encourage your spirit. Now when you see someone else in a situation, speak an encouraging word over them. It is good when you can speak over your life, but it is great when you can encourage someone in their situation. It is so powerful how speaking words out of our mouths can change the outcome of somebody else. Be encouraged, and then go out and encourage somebody else's situation. Go and get God's word in you, and then speak it over your life. Encourage your marriage, encourage your children, and encourage your family, your friends, your church, and your Pastor. Remember that God's word is your greatest encourager. You can stand against anything that the enemy throws at your life. I want you to believe in God. Jesus Christ is the Word of God. Whenever you speak His Word, you are speaking to Him in every situation in your life. When Jesus died on the cross, on the third day, He rose with all power in His hands. The same power that Jesus Christ has is that same power that He has given to us. Just believe in him. Speak the word, and watch it change your life.

KEYS TO ENCOURAGE YOURSELF DAILY

- Meditate on God's Word Daily
- Speak and declare God's Word over your life
- Pray without ceasing
- Surround yourself with those of high Faith
- Remember your authority in Christ
- Remember Past Victories
- Release negative toxic thoughts
- Find time to engage in activities that bring you joy and happiness

SCRIPTURES FOR ENCOURAGEMENT

- Proverbs 3:5,6 Trust in The Lord with all thine heart and lean not unto thine own understanding. In all thy ways acknowledge him, and he shall direct thy paths.
- Proverbs 18:10 The name of The Lord is a strong tower; the righteous runneth into it and is safe.
- Isaiah 41:10 Fear thou not; for I am with thee: I will strengthen thee; yea, I will help thee; yea, I will uphold thee with the right hand of my righteousness.
- John 14:27 Peace I leave with you, my peace I give unto you; not as the world giveth, give I unto you. Let not your heart be troubled, neither let it be afraid.
- John 16:33 These things I have spoken unto you, that in me ye shall have peace. In the world ye shall have tribulation: but be of good cheer; I have overcome the world.

PRAYER OF ENCOURAGEMENT

Father, I come to you in the name of Jesus Christ. Father, those who are reading right now, I speak an encouraging word over their lives. Right now, in the name of Jesus Christ, I curse any demonic attack or hindrance upon their lives. Let the Holy Ghost arrest the works of the enemy. I speak they are blessed, healed, delivered, and set free by the power in your word. I speak they are the head and not the tail, above and not beneath. I speak that the plan you have for their life will come to pass. In Jesus' name, Amen!

Are you honest with God about the depths of your pain? Hopelessness, confusion, anger, depression?

_____

_____

_____

_____

_____

_____

_____

_____

_____

_____

_____

_____

_____

_____

_____

_____

_____

_____

_____

_____

_____

_____

_____

_____

_____

What do you do to encourage yourself in the Lord?

_____

_____

_____

_____

_____

_____

_____

_____

_____

_____

_____

_____

_____

_____

_____

_____

_____

_____

_____

_____

_____

_____

CHAPTER 10

RECEIVE THE BLESSING OF GOD

Receiving the blessings of God is a privilege that all Christians should be grateful for. We are blessed every day, and we should always remember to be thankful. When you receive a blessing from God, it means that he has done something good for you. The Bible says that God gives us many blessings because He loves us and wants to show us His love in a variety of ways. Blessings come in many forms: He may give you money or food when you are hungry or poor, He may give you good health when you are sick, He may protect you from danger and keep you safe from harm, or He may give you peace when there is war or trouble in your life (Psalm 16:7).

It is important to remember that receiving the blessings of God does not mean that we will never experience pain or suffering again; rather, it means that through these trials, God will help us grow stronger in our faith and learn how to rely on Him; more than ever before!

There are five things that God wants you to have after you speak it and believe it. God wants to show you how to *RECEIVE IT!* The five things He wants you to receive are Obedience, Integrity, Trust, Discernment, and Giving.

Let's start with obedience; this is one of the toughest for some Christians to achieve. A lot of times, we won't spend enough time hearing from God. So when God leads us to do something that we could be blessed by, we don't know the voice of directions. Our God is very specific; we must always follow His instructions. Then and only then will we be able to receive the blessing. The bible says that obedience is better than sacrifice. So it doesn't matter how much you think you know or do if you are not obedient to God's word, it can't work for you.

The second blessing is Integrity. This means the quality of being honest and having strong moral principles and moral uprightness. One thing we must always do is be honest. When we are not operating in integrity, then no one can trust us, and God can't trust you either. We must be responsible for our life, how we treat others, and how we treat God's word. No one likes a liar or someone they can't trust. We must make sure that we keep our integrity intact and walk upright before God and men. We are ambassadors of Jesus Christ; when people see us, they must see Christ in us. People watch to see how you live. When you live foul and make promises that you can't keep, make sure you make it right with the person you made promises to! Sure sometimes things come up, and your intentions were not right. Maybe something fell through, and you were not honest with an individual; go to the person and explain your actions and true intent. Ask for forgiveness; therefore, you will have kept your integrity. Never say anything and then turn around and do the opposite. Always keep your word to God and man, and both will bless you.

The third is Trust. Trust means to have a firm belief in the reliability, truth, ability, or strength of someone or something. When someone trusts you, it means they can rely on you. Ask yourself, are you reliable? Can people depend on you? Can you be trusted? In these days and times, we are living in, it seems like trust is gone out the window. Sometimes you will trust people with secrets that are dear to their hearts believing that they operate in truth and integrity. It's disturbing and troublesome to discover that the people you trusted with secrets betray you and reveal your innermost thoughts to the world. When people trust you, they relinquish the hidden part of their hearts to you. They let down their guard to receive help from you.

To only find out that they can't trust you is betrayal. The worst thing in the world to me is an untrustworthy Christian, and there shouldn't be one. We should be there for our brother and sister in Christ! There are even Pastors that the flock can't be trusted. They do not possess the qualities of Christ. Many in the body of Christ have problems, issues, and burdens they carry, and yet they are afraid to go to their own Pastor because they do not operate with integrity and have broken the trust of those that they lead. There are also many Pastors who keep a lot inside and have trouble as well sharing how they feel, and they are human too. They have flaws and issues just like anyone else. They also need an outlet or a confidant, someone they can confide in. We need to know that when we make our lives available to anyone, they should be able to trust us. Now, what about God? Can he trust you? Can He rely on you to do what he has called you to do? He needs to know that he can bless you, and you will still follow him. He needs to know that if all hell is breaking loose around you, you know He will bring you out of it. He wants you to know that if you need anything, he is a provider.

The fourth thing is discernment; it is the process of determining God's desire in a situation or for one's life. You have to have this! The bible says in Habakkuk 2:3 For the vision is yet for an appointed time, but at the end, it shall speak, and not lie: though it tarry, wait for it; because it will surely come, it will not tarry. You see, you have to understand the time or season you are in. If God has given you a promise, it will surely come to pass. You have to know the right time. You must know what to do when the time comes. You must know who and not who to share the promise with. All of this is discernment. You can only get that through prayer, fasting, and his word. Prayer brings on a relationship. When you pray, God guides you on when it's time to wait or when it is time to move. Fasting denies the flesh from making carnal decisions, and it keeps you more focused on God than on the situation. In fact, some answers don't come but by fasting and prayer. Now when you add God's word to the equation, which is Jesus, you can have clarity in what you need to do, who you need to see, and where you need to go. When you have good discernment, the enemy can't keep a foothold on your life. You will know when to stand still. Get good discernment, and you will receive the blessing of God

The Fifth is giving, and this means to freely transfer the possession of something to someone, hand over to. In order for you to receive, you must give. Giving isn't always money; that is what people recognize it the most for. There are many ways to give. You can give of your time. When you donate your time to God or do his will, it opens up ways of blessings for you. It shows God that you are putting him before anything else. Considering time is valuable, we must make sure we use it wisely. There is a saying that time waits for no one. When you give time in church, bible study, and give your time to help others, there is no possible way that God won't bless you. Give of yourself and watch God move for you. Now let's talk about giving in money. So many people don't believe in giving, but if you don't give in money, you won't be able to receive money. The purpose of giving is that you experience no lack. If a man lacks something, it is usually his lack of giving. When you give at church, it helps bring the church on one accord; it also helps the mission of the church. Giving also helps you think of someone else before you think of yourself. Giving is an action word, just like love is.

You show love when giving. When you give money, you further the gospel of Jesus Christ. This is how you should give cheerfully, willingly, not grudgingly, purposefully. God gave his Son to us; why can't we give ourselves resources and time. If you do all these things, surely God will bless you, and you will receive the blessings of God. I pray that this book will bless you. Remember to read his word, take time to study, and let the word get down in your soul. Quote it, memorize it, think it, believe in it. Obey the Word and confess it. Then when it becomes you, it will change your very life. The word is alive; it is the living word. Speak it, Believe It, Receive It.

God has blessed us with so many wonderful things, and we are so grateful for them. We believe God wants us to be joyful, healthy, and whole. He gives us the power to make our lives better. We can see evidence of His blessings everywhere we look, from the beautiful flowers in our backyard to the stars that shine at night in the sky.

When life tries to discourage you and make you feel that God is not with you, remind yourself daily You are blessed and highly favored. You have been blessed with a life, and you have been blessed with the ability to live that life in a way that allows you to make choices and decisions, to have experiences, and learn from them. You have been given this gift of a world that is yours to explore, and you have been given the ability to make it better. The world has never been perfect, but it can be made more perfect—and it is up to us all to make that happen.

As we go through life, many things will challenge us and test us; some things will be easy and others difficult. But even in these challenging moments, we must remember that God's love is always with us, and His blessings surround us at every moment of our lives. We must never forget that we are never alone! We are not meant for this world alone—we were created for eternity with God in Heaven! That is why He sent His son Jesus Christ into this world: so that we could be saved from death and sin forevermore!

As we go through life, we should focus on receiving God's blessings instead of focusing on what's missing in our lives. When we focus on how blessed we are, it helps us to be more grateful for all that we have—and it makes us want to do good things for others who may not have as much as they need or deserve. You have power, and you are an overcomer. You are well able to live the life you want. You can achieve what people think you can't achieve. What are you going to believe?

KEYS TO RECEIVING THE BLESSINGS OF GOD

- Seek first the Kingdom of God
- Humble yourself to the hand of God
- Repent to God and change for the better
- Hunger and thirst after the things of God
- Understand that God is the Source of All blessings
- Discern fertile soil and sow seeds
- Keep Gods commandments
- Declare God's Word over your life

SCRIPTURES TO RECEIVE GODS' BLESSINGS

- **Deuteronomy 30:19** Today, I have given you a choice between life and death, between blessings and curses. Now I call on heaven and earth to witness the choice you make. Oh, that you would choose life so that you and your descendants might live!

- **James 1:17** Every good gift and every perfect gift is from above and cometh down from the Father of lights, with whom is no variableness, neither shadow of turning

- **2nd Corinthians 9:8** And God is able to make all grace abound toward you; that ye, always having all sufficiency in all things, may abound to every good work:

- **Ephesians 1:3** Blessed be the God and Father of our Lord Jesus Christ, who hath blessed us with all spiritual blessings in heavenly places in Christ

PRAYER TO RECEIVE THE BLESSINGS OF GOD

Father, in the name of Jesus, we come unto you, and we thank you for the blessing. You are the blessing God, for you told us to first seek ye the kingdom of God, and all these things will be added unto us. So because we seek you, the benefits of God are on our lives. We receive everything that you have for us. We ask that you give us the wisdom and the knowledge to know how to move with the blessing of our life. Father, we are so grateful that you love us to the point of even allowing us to have it. We love you, and we thank you that the blessing of the Lord is on us and we receive in Jesus' name.

What does it mean to you to be blessed by God? What are some ways that God has blessed you?

_____

_____

_____

_____

_____

_____

_____

_____

_____

_____

_____

_____

_____

_____

_____

_____

_____

_____

_____

_____

_____

_____

_____

Write down ways that God can use you to bless others.

_____

_____

_____

_____

_____

_____

_____

_____

_____

_____

_____

_____

_____

_____

_____

_____

_____

_____

_____

_____

_____

_____

_____

_____

_____

_____

_____

CHAPTER 11

LIVING IN THE OVERFLOW

What if I told you that there's a way to experience total and complete abundance in your life? Life is full of blessings, but we forget them. We get caught up in the pursuit of things and forget that they aren't the point. That they can never fill us up or bring us true happiness as God has intended for us. But what if I told you that God had given you the blueprint to make sure those blessings stick with you? What if I told you that it's possible to make sure your heart stays open, that your mind stays soft, and that your expectations stay high in expectancy of God's overflow? It's all about renewing your mind daily, transforming your heart, and developing a mentality and expectation of abundance. Until we truly know it's God's will for us to live above life's limits, we won't.

When you're living in the overflow of God's love, affection, and blessings, you already know what's important: your faith, speaking God's Word, believing God's Word, and receiving God's Word. You're not just, you're not just thriving, but you are *LIVING IN THE OVERFLOW* of God. When you know that everything is going to be all right, no matter what happens tomorrow or next week, or next year, you can relax in God, knowing that he will care for you. God loves us so much that He will always be there for us when we need Him most. And because He loves us so much, He wants us to know how loved we are so that we don't forget about all of His blessings when times get tough! Live in the OVERFLOW of God.

The overflow of God's love, affection, and blessings is still available to us, but we must be willing to receive them. We have to open up our hearts and minds to His plan for our lives. Isaiah 55:1-2 says: "Come, all you who are thirsty, come to the waters; and you who have no money, come, buy and eat! Come buy wine and milk without money and without cost." The only way we can live in this overflow is by accepting Jesus Christ as our Lord and Savior. Jesus said in John 14:6, "I am the way, the truth, and the life. No one comes to the Father except through me. We know that all things work together for good for those who love God (Romans 8:28). If we love Him, then everything he gives us will work out in our favor because He loves us too!

Live your life in a state of overflow. You have been given everything you need to live a joyful life, and it's time to stop letting your worries hold you back from living up to your full potential.

Live up to your full potential, let go of your fears, worries, and anxiety about what other people think about you, and focus on the love God has for you. God's Word is true, and there is no good thing that he will withhold from you. God desires you to have the overflow of His blessings and enjoy the fullness of life greater than what we have ever imagined. God wants us to experience life in abundance. It's the very reason Jesus came to the earth. John 10:10 Jesus said, "I came that they may have and enjoy life, and have it in abundance (to the full, till it overflows)

You are loved by God, who made you and knew you better than anyone else ever could. Remember this truth as soon as possible each day: I am loved by God. That is all that matters. God has given you a life of blessings, abundance, and overflow. Ephesians 3:20 states as He showers you with uncommon favor, you will walk in the reality of His overflow. He is able to do exceedingly, abundantly above all that we ask or think " He is the God of the overflow

There is never a shortage of what God will provide; there are no limits to the depths to which he will go for you, and there is no shortage of His resources. However, there is often a shortage of believing and faith on our part in understanding the magnitude of His goodness. In order for each and every one of us to totally experience this type of goodness, we have to renew our minds daily, transform our hearts, and develop a mentality and expectation of abundance. Until we truly know it's God's will for us to live above life's limits, we won't. Take the limits off God and grab hold of His promises.

Sometimes we can get caught up in the abundance or overflow that can be seen physically or monetarily sense, and scripture does talk about abundance in wealth, food, and necessity. There is another type of abundance and overflow that is often overlooked: the abundance of grace. Grace is the unmerited favor of God towards those who do not deserve it. In other words, grace is God giving us what we don't deserve and forgiving us for our sins. The Scriptures tell us that "God has poured out his love into our hearts by the Holy Spirit" (Romans 5:5). This statement tells us what happens when we receive this kind of grace from God—it overflows into our lives! Our hearts are filled with His love, which causes us to love Him more than anything else in this world; and that kind of love brings about good works because it comes from deep within our hearts instead of being forced upon us by someone else or by fear (James 2:17).

What about spiritual abundance? What about the gifts of the Spirit and spiritual growth and maturity? These are more than just the tools that God gives us to help us achieve our goals; they are part of our very essence as believers. We can have all that we need because He has given us all things to enjoy (John 10:10). The Spirit Himself will lead you into truth (John 16:13). You can live abundantly because God has ordained that you should live in peace with Him (Colossians 3:15). It's not about making more money or having more sex or living longer— it's about living abundantly as a child of God who is loved and cared for by the Father who wants nothing but the best for his children! God's gifts and fruit are intended for us to enjoy. His provision is perfect for our needs, and He has given us an abundance of spiritual resources to help us in our walk with Him.

Living in the overflow means we know that we don't have to be afraid because God has already brought us through all kinds of situations before. He knows exactly what we need, when we need it and why and He will take care of us no matter what happens. As you walk in and live in the overflow, you know that God loves us so much that He sent His Son Jesus Christ to take on human flesh so that we could be saved from sin by His death on the cross and resurrection three days later. It means knowing that we can trust Him completely with our lives because He has proven Himself faithful to us over and over again throughout history! When we are living in the overflow, we have a clear vision of who God is and what He wants from us. We know that He has given us all we need to walk out our purpose, and when we walk in that purpose with Him, we are empowered by His Spirit to be who He created us to be. We have hope for the future because we know that God is at work in each of our lives—and He will continue to do so until His purposes are fulfilled. *WELCOME TO YOUR NEXT SEASON OF THE OVERFLOW!!!!!*

KEYS TO LIVING IN THE OVERFLOW OF GOD

- Spend time with God in prayer
- Submit every area of your life unto God and ask God to Saturate those areas
- Declare Gods Word
- Operating in God's laws of sowing and reaping
- Honor Gods Prophets
- Develop a heart of thanksgiving
- Develop a mentality of abundance and expectation
- Speak and Believe by Faith
- Serve Others

SCRIPTURES TO LIVING IN THE OVERFLOW

- **Psalm 23:1 (NIV)** The Lord is my shepherd; I lack nothing.

- **Psalm 37:4 (NIV)** Delight yourself in the Lord, and he will give you the desires of your heart.

- **Deuteronomy 8:18 (NIV)** Remember the Lord your God, for it is he who gives you the ability to produce wealth and so confirms his covenant.

- **Proverbs 10:22 (NIV)** The blessing of the Lord brings wealth, and he adds no trouble to it.

- **Psalm 37:25 (NIV)** I was young, and now I am old, yet I have never seen the righteous forsaken or their children begging bread.

PRAYER TO LIVING IN THE OVERFLOW

Father, in the name of Jesus, we thank you again for your promises. We thank you for restoring us through your word. We can now walk with no limitations because we have taken the limits of our life. However, you want to bless me; I am willing to receive thank you for blessing us with more than enough. We are walking in total abundance. We are walking in the fullness of your prosperity. All that we ever dreamed of is ours now. Your blessings have overtaken us, and we are walking in more than enough. More in finances, wealth, health, and abundance. Father God, thank you for the overflow in Jesus' name

How do negative thoughts and actions prohibit you from you experiencing God's blessing and walking in abundance?

_____

_____

_____

_____

_____

_____

_____

_____

_____

_____

_____

_____

_____

_____

_____

_____

_____

_____

_____

_____

_____

_____

_____

_____

_____

_____

_____

Describe a moment in your life when you experienced the abundance and overflow of God?

_____

_____

_____

_____

_____

_____

_____

_____

_____

_____

_____

_____

_____

_____

_____

_____

_____

_____

_____

_____

_____

_____

_____

_____

_____

_____

ABOUT THE AUTHOR

RONNIE WILSON

Ronnie Wilson was born in Williamston, North Carolina. He is a Pastor, Psalmist, Author, and Entrepreneur. He has a love for God and a passion for God's people. He is an Elder in the Church of Christ, Disciple of Christ International. He has been in the ministry for over ten years. He still resides in his hometown of Williamston, NC. Ronnie believes that people are the world's greatest asset. Ronnie Wilson believes in Jesus Christ. He believes that there is no way to heaven without him. Ronnie Wilson cares about people, and he loves ministering to them. He believes that love conquers all things. Ronnie believes that through Jesus Christ and encouragement, we can conquer all things. He believes that he is called to preach the gospel of Jesus Christ. He wants to be an effective leader, and he wants to be able to reach the masses. He does all these things in the name of Jesus Christ.